AF470220

BETTY BOOP™
99
Secrets

First published in 2010 by Blue Sky Books Ltd
2nd Floor, Berkeley Square House, Berkeley Square, London W1J 6BD
www.blueskybooks.co.uk

British Cataloguing-in-Publication Data:
A catalogue record of this book is available from the British Library.

ISBN 978-1-907309-03-8

Designed by Spirit Design Consultants, London
www.spirit-design.com

Editorial contribution: Sacha Markin

Printed and bound in China through Printworks Int. Ltd.

The secret's out –
Betty Boop
shares all!

Call your friends; you've got
a date... Boop-oop-a-doop!

1

Pop on your favourite music getting ready – something lively. Oh, is that the time?

Wear something you feel great in. 'Mirror mirror on the wall, who's the prettiest of them all? Oh, why it's me!'

Give yourself plenty of time to get ready, you want to look your best! No, you don't need the day off work.

Don't wear heels too high on your first date, unless you know he's tall – give him some kind of chance!

Treat yourself to a cute new outfit, even a whole new look – wow, what are you doing tonight?

B-U-T please don't wait 'til the very last minute to go shopping – panic stations – no thank you!

Easy on the make-up – remember it's a first date, don't scare him away. Hey, come back, it's only lipstick!

What do you want from the date? A little fun or something more, find out if he wants the same thing – doesn't that make sense?

Please, please! No talking marriage on a first date – oh, you do want him on the first plane out of here.

Keep the extra-gooey lip gloss for another time or he could be stuck on you – I mean really stuck on you, get off please!

Try something different, if it's sunny, how about a picnic? Sounds sweet, ice-cream?

Love in Cyber-Space, oh, do I need a helmet? Get an on-line name that's fun, sexy and easy to remember. Mine? Why, Miss Betty Boop!

If you blush easy, put a little extra base foundation on – is it warm in here?

Look good, feel great. One last look in the mirror... go knock 'em dead.

SMELL DELICIOUS! Wearing your favourite scent is part of the fun – spray away!

Not dated for a while, don't worry sweetie, like walking on heels; it just takes a little practice. What's keeping you? Go!

Meet for lunch, instead of dinner – it's easier to get away if it's not going well – now where is that door?

You sure you can walk in those shoes? Oh, I see, you do want to fall head over heels for him – crash-bang-ouch!

Look smart – be smart! Tell a friend where you're going, take your phone and meet in public. Betty gold-tip – have fun, be safe!

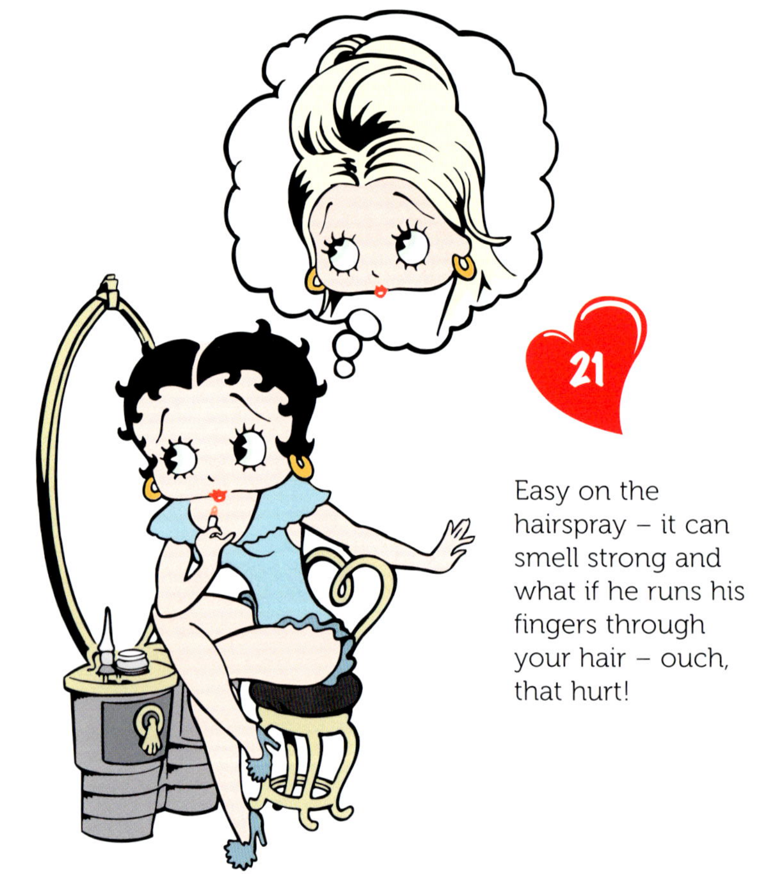

21

Easy on the hairspray – it can smell strong and what if he runs his fingers through your hair – ouch, that hurt!

A beautiful stranger... or just downright strange? Check in with friends on any blind dates they fix up for you. So, tell me a little bit more about this guy.

Never wear new shoes on a first date. Oh, you can glide across the room in toe-crunchers! Ouch!

Nobody's perfect, don't be too picky, get to know him a little more, you may be surprised – why those depths aren't so hidden!

Let him book the table and open doors – everyone loves a gent. Boop-oop-a-doop!

You can keep your date waiting a little and don't turn up early – after all, it's what we ladies do.

B-U-T! Don't be too late – he might think you've stood him up and leave before you get there. Dinner for one?

Remember; be confident, boys like it... so they tell me... Oops, Sssshhh

A no show? If your date stands you up, second chances are a no-no! I'm sorry but you should have thought about that, good bye!

If he pays you a compliment, say thank you – this boy's got taste!

If you're blind date is less than gorgeous, you can still be polite, stay a few minutes and then make your excuses... I'm sorry, but... uhhm, I've got to go!

Remember it is just a date. He may be the one, but if he isn't you can still have a good time!

Really – his idea of a great first date is a TV football game and pizza – what are you waiting for, get out quick... and no, you can't take the pizza with you!

Does he need the number of a good optician? Then why are his eyes roaming around the room – no, no, no!

Play it cool – he may be the most gorgeous thing you've ever seen, but you don't have to pounce!

Keep your first date short. Leave him wishing for more, not wanting to escape!

D-A-T-E A-L-E-R-T – If he brings his mother along... say "hello ma'am, nice to meet you," then take your shoes off and run!

Does he smell yummy? Ooh, I think he might be good enough to eat!

Don't be afraid to cut it short if it's not working – life really is too short, you could be shopping!

G-O-O-D S-I-G-N – your knees go weak, your palms sweat, and your tummy does flip flops (For all the right reasons).

B-A-D S-I-G-N – your knees go weak, your palms sweat, and your tummy does flip flops (For all the wrong reasons).

Love is all around you... there are lots of places you can meet your dream man – the supermarket, the deli, an art gallery, parties, the swimming pool – they leave the house too you know!

Give him a chance – he may be nervous – well, you are gorgeous.

8 FT.

He says he can only see you Tuesdays because he's dating other girls – bye-bye-baby, baby good-bye!

BE YOURSELF. Don't be something you're not – why would you, you're perfect as you are!

Eye contact is great, just don't over do it – hello... hello... I think she's in a trance!

The day after a date, never wait by the phone for your date to call – go out and enjoy yourself.

The same gestures are a good sign things are going well. Was that a kiss he just blew, there you go, here's one back – catch!

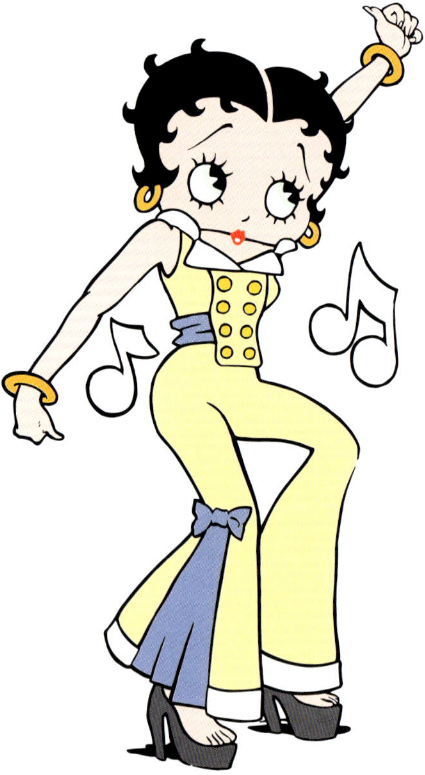

49

Have fun – that's what dates are about – smile, laugh, dance – wow, he hasn't taken his eyes off you once.

Get to know all about him. Ask him lots and lots of questions.

B-U-T. If he doesn't ask one question about you – say goodbye. My mother warned me about men like that...

Make eye contact... it tells him you're interested. Well, he is very sweet – wink, wink.

Sip your drink slowly and watch him fall for you.

Does he give you butterflies... well, he could be the one.

Listening is very attractive... please tell me more!

Remember, being single can be fun too... enjoy it!

Lean in towards him when you're chatting – i-r-r-e-s-i-s-t-a-b-l-e!

Good dating signs – you think about him a lot, there's chemistry, you don't look at anyone else and you look forward to seeing him – I say... don't let him go!

Chatted the night away. Time's flown. Got a lot in common – Maybe this date is the first of many! Saturday? Oh, I think I'm free Saturday, let me check.

He's absolutely delicious... if you really hit it off – steal a kiss. This boy is too good to be true.

Say his name when you're talking – he'll melt in your hands.

Try not to interrupt your date... good manners are very attractive.

You can't hurry love! (But you can give it a little nudge... I had a lovely evening, we must do this again some time!)

DATE HEAVEN – if you had a really great time, tell him so!

Skip the movies on a first date – let him concentrate on you! Coo-ey, I'm over here!

K is for K-I-S-S-I-N-G. They either can or they can't – I'm keeping my fingers crossed!

He has female friends (that he doesn't kiss), that's a good sign – he gets on with girls.

Your love bomb just bombed, call up the girls and have a night out, you'll forget him in no time – boop-oop-a-doop!

Don't call him by your ex boyfriend's name – unless that's his name too! Ooops

A lady's instincts are never wrong – trust them! I knew there was something not quite right about that man.

Never ever say a bad word about his mother – unless you don't want to see him again!

Did you know, our eyebrows rise and fall when we meet someone we like and theirs do too! Why, hello sailor.

BE POLITE. Don't answer your mobile phone during a date – unless you really have to.

SS
BOOP

Smile a lot... it's nice to be friendly.

If you're on a first date and not having fun, let him go! There's someone out there who'll love those jokes of his!!!

Safety first – meet in public till you know him well.

The dance floor is great for flirting. Shake what your mama gave you!

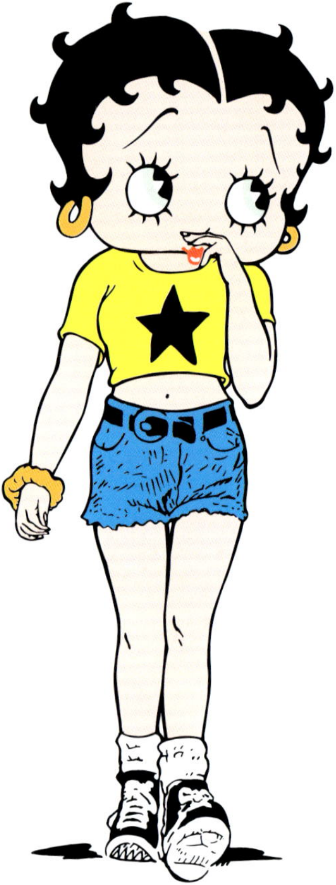

He says he likes you just the way you are – that really is sweet!

Playing with your hair is very flirty – now what were you saying, oh that's right you think I'm B-O-O-P-I-F-U-L!

You're right, you didn't sign up for the whole gang? If he arrives with his posse, hot foot it out of there!

If he makes you're heart beat faster, flirt away – smile, laugh, talk softly, touch him gently on the arm, he's hanging off your every word!

How are his manners? Generous gent or something else I'd rather not repeat? Yikes – where's the fire escape?

A sign he's taking things too quickly – he's set up camp outside your house – out the back door quick!

Mr Wrong will never be Mr Right!

Golden Rule: be yourself – be fantastic, funny and charming – well you are, aren't you?

Don't be sad if he's not Mr. Right. There are lots more fish in the sea. That's it, cast your line... oh, what've you got there... tasty.

Let your date treat you – you're worth it, aren't you?

Sssshhh. Try not to say 'We must do this again some time,' if you know there will never be date number two.

Come and get me! When he has to chase you, he's much less likely to fly away.

D-A-T-E A-L-E-R-T. He's not sure if he's single... is he sure he saw you leave?

If Mr Right turns out to be Mr No-Way Jose, put it in the bad date diary and move on. Tomorrow is another day.

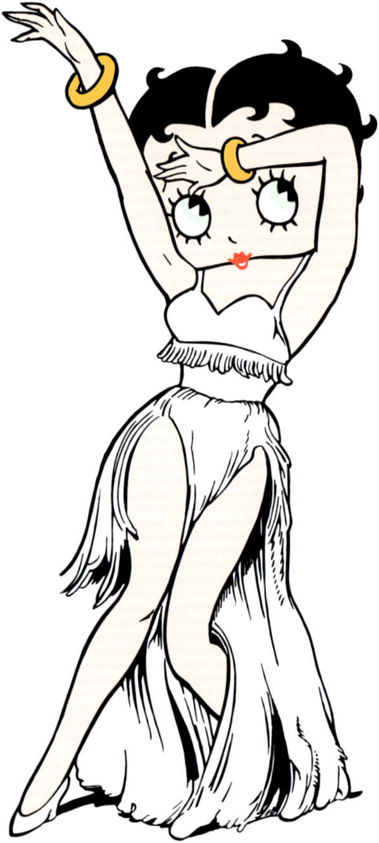

Don't tell him everything about yourself; leave a little mystery... just call me Betty...

If he doesn't call you, it can only be because he lost your number. 'Next please!'

No go dates – anybody who doesn't make you laugh – well we need to giggle, right!

He wants to see you again (why wouldn't he!), think of something fun and different for date number two!

The body doesn't lie, so be careful what you say – no folded arms please!

I'm sorry sweetie, but you may have to kiss a lot of frogs before you find your prince – Yelp!

If you want to meet Mr Right, please get out of the house! Put on your favourite dress, hit the town and have some fun – he's out there somewhere.

99

You're special – don't ever settle for second best! Promise?

Love,
Betty x

Betty Boop™

Look out for more secrets from **Betty Boop...**

Beauty

How do you get super-luscious lashes? Boop-a-licious lips? The tan-fantastic? Read on and you'll find out.

New You

We all need a boost from time to time. Miss Boop shows us lots of little things that make a very big difference. Juicy fruit drinks, sunny thoughts and healthy tips for a New You, you'll love!

Happiness

Being happy is easier than you think! Think lovely, warm, fresh towels. A cosy picnic for two. Falling in love – ahhh. Secrets to make you and everybody else happy, too!